Dog Books for Kids

By K. Bennett
Mendon Cottage Books

JD-Biz Publishing

**Download Free Books!
http://MendonCottageBooks.com**

All Rights Reserved.

No part of this publication may be reproduced in any form or by any means, including scanning, photocopying, or otherwise without prior written permission from JD-Biz Corp. Copyright © 2015. All Images Licensed by Fotolia and 123RF.

Read More Amazing Animal Books

Purchase at Amazon.com

Download Free Books!
http://MendonCottageBooks.com

Table of Contents

Introduction 4

    Chapter 1 7

        Chapter 2 12

    Chapter 3 21

        Conclusion 26

Author Bio 28

Publisher 33

Introduction

Happiness is a warm puppy.
— *Charles M. Schulz*

Boxers are fun loving dogs with a heart of gold. At first glance, they may seem imposing with a hidden message of 'see but don't touch' — that is until their joy and boundless energy comes shining through!

This short haired, stocky breed comes from Germany. A mix between an Old English Bulldog and the Bullenbeisser (Now extinct), this breed is a part of the working group of dogs. After World War I, Boxers arrived to the United States, and became a lovable companion to many dog owners.

Despite their origins, it is not a surprise to hear Boxers called the "Peter Pan" of the dog world. This label is quite accurate because this breed of dog takes a long time to mature into adulthood. Usually they are considered mature when they are three years old! So, you will enjoy their puppy like antics for a few years.

Typical Boxers are smart, funny, alert and loyal. They are also friendly, (although wary with strangers until they warm up) and will go to great lengths to please you. However, it is important to note these wonderful qualities hide a stubborn streak that could outlast your patience! Thankfully, this type of behavior is not common, and is the result of inappropriate training methods.

Mental and physical exercise is required for this breed. This does not mean he / she cannot live in an apartment with you. They can adapt as long as you are there to spend time with them and provide the required exercise.

This breed is gentle with children and a wonderful playmate for them. Boxers also love hugs, pats, kisses and rubs. The more the merrier! There is no doubt their clownish behavior, goofy antics, crazy faces and boundless energy will bring a smile to your face, and a warm feeling to your heart.

For these reasons and more, Boxers are highly recommended as a loyal companion well deserving of the title… *man's best friend*!

Chapter 1

An interesting start – 16th century

Boxers have a very interesting history spanning many years. The AKC notes their history may extend as far back as the 16th century. In those days, boxers had a different appearance, but their descendants were no less noble than the breed we know today. Why is that?

Well, there is enough evidence for us to conclude boxers are descendants from the fighting dogs found in the valleys of Tibet. Then, the Germans played a hand in refining the breed and developing the amazing qualities we know today. Boxers are also cousins to the Bulldog breeds and have beautiful coats in fantastic colors!

Artist impressions during the 16th and 17th century detailed dogs, which look like our modern day Boxer. But the resemblance does not stop there. The Spanish Alano and Perro de Presa appear to have some relation to the Boxer as well or is at least a common ancestor.

In France there is another breed known as Dogue de Bordeaux similar to the Tibetan Mastiff. Bouldogue de Mida came from this breed and you will note Boxers have many characteristics from this dog. But, these are not the only dogs that share ancestry with Boxers. Add some Terrier into the mix and you will have a well-rounded Boxer dog!

The ancestry and origins of the Boxer proves what a beautiful mix this breed has become. Although the AKC registered Boxers in 1904, it took a few more years (1940's) for Americans to fully appreciate this amazing dog!

To think about: Boxers shed, shed and shed some more! If you have allergies, you need to take this characteristic into account. Why? Because, more than likely you will find hair on your floor, couch, chair, clothes, and everything else!

Note of advice: Brushing the coat of your Boxer is a great way to keep the shedding down. You may want to do it a couple times during the week (Occasional is recommended) to get rid of loose hair. If not, it will fall out in places you may not necessarily like!

A dog by any other name…

Boxers love children and can spend all day playing with them. They love to play with you too! And this feeling can manifest itself in cute ways like sitting on your lap, brushing against you for a tummy pat, or a giant hug. Being next to you is the dearest thing to a Boxer's heart, and they will not hesitate to show their affection in adorable ways.

Boxers are very active and always moving around. They are here, there and everywhere, so expect them to get into every nook and cranny! This means if you do not give them the proper exercise, they will find creative ways to get busy. This can cause you a bit of a headache, especially if they chew on your favorite pair of shoes.

Mental stimulation is also needed for this breed. You may wonder why this is required when the Boxer is such a friendly pet. The **Njspca.org** article written by Dana Goldberg helps us to understand the particular characteristics you need to know when it comes to Boxers. Consider the following details:

Boxers are not really guard dogs! You may find that surprising when you consider their appearance, but the website notes this breed is more of a watchdog than a precise guard dog. What is the difference? In one word: Aggressiveness.

Boxers do not have much (if any) aggressive bones in their body. Of course there may be exceptions to this rule, but this is the general disposition of the breed. Many seem to agree with this assessment. When a poll asked owners what their Boxer was like, the response was simple and sweet: A clown dog!

And when someone tries to teach a boxer to be a good guard dog, they soon find they have 'bitten off more than they can chew.' They may also give up in despair concluding the effort is a waste of time.

Ultimately, Boxers are playful, funny, loving and kind. It should be noted they do have a stubborn streak, which may reflect itself in interesting ways. This simply means they will ignore you until they feel like paying attention! To avoid this behavior, obedience training is a great way to go. As the website notes: "This is a win-win situation for both you and your pet."

Note: It is important to note Boxers do receive training as guardians, and they are protective of their family. However, by nature this breed is not an all-out aggressive dog and it is not vicious.

 # Chapter 2

Now you know what a Boxer is like and its origins, so let us examine some of its features:

In review: Boxers have a unique personality. They have been around for a long time, and require both physical and mental exercise. They are great watchdogs, but not necessarily guard dogs.

They love to sit in your lap, and require warm attention. Their boisterous nature will bring a smile to your face and leave you wanting more.

They are not a friend of extreme weather conditions, and do not like to be bored. And, if you leave them to their own devices for a long time, they will find very creative ways to get busy!

As a whole, Boxers make wonderful companions for a loving home.

FUN FACTS FOR KIDS:

Boxers do not only have unique personalities, but also unique tricks! Some of these are called the "**kidney beaning**" and the "**woo – woo**". Do you know what these terms are, and what it means? Ask your parents or a guardian to help you research the answer online!

- *How much can they weigh?* The male can weigh approximately 66-70 pounds, and the female can weigh approximately 55-60 pounds. This doesn't mean a Boxer can't weigh more / less than this, but this is the standard weight.

-*How tall can they get?* A male can reach 23 – 25 inches in height, and a female can get to 21.5 – 23.5 inches in height.

-*What about babies?* Boxer litters are average in size. The female can have between 6 – 8 puppies.

-*How long to they live?* Lifespan is usually between 9 - 10 years.

-*What about their coat?* They have a smooth coat that sits tightly to the body. It is short haired and shiny.

-*How often do they shed?* Quite a bit! If you suffer from allergies, this is something to consider.

-*What color are they?* Boxers are beautiful dogs with a distinctive look. Fawn and Brindle are known and popular colors. However, White and Albino can also be found. Interestingly enough 20-25 % of all Boxer pups are born white, but those dogs which are light-skinned can be affected by sunlight. It is also interesting to note Boxers do not carry a gene for a solid black coat.

- *What about their temperament or personality?* As noted Boxers have an amazing personality. They do not like strangers and will bark, but when it comes to family they are all heart.

They are intelligent and cheerful. They are also honest and loyal and happy to spend time with you. There is a degree of headstrong and stubborn tendencies that could apply, but this is due to inappropriate obedience training. This can be corrected by taking the nature of the Boxer into account and choosing the right professional help, if you are unable to handle the training yourself.

Caring for your Boxer

Boxers are not only our pets, but also valued members of our home. So, we want to be sure they get proper care and like most, if not all of us, the right diet and exercise is important.

Let us begin with the right diet:

Gauging how much your dog should eat is a good place to start. If you notice your pet may be getting a little too heavy, cut back on the food intake. If you notice too little weight, then increase the portions of food.

So how can you be sure if your dog is being fed correctly? The same principle applies for other breeds, but this general rule of thumb is a nice way to test your animal to see how well you are feeding him.

Try the following test listed on **dogtime.com** at home. Are you ready?

FIRST: Put your thumbs on his spine and run your fingers along the side of the Boxers body.

SECOND: Once there, feel for his ribs beneath the muscle. If you can see them, he needs more food! If you cannot feel them (Too many rolls of fat), you need to put him / her on a diet.

Mealtime

Allboxerinfo.com notes the following recommendations: The food you feed your puppy will not only affect its health and growth but also its behavior. And with an adult boxer, the food you feed it will not only affect its health but also its life span. So feeding is more than just making sure your dog doesn't starve! With this idea in mind, you want to make the best choice for your pet.

This website recommends home cooked meals for your puppy. If you choose to buy manufactured food, choose a high quality brand and add milk. The recommended amount is 1 part to 3 parts. This "soupy mix" will allow the puppy to easily digest the meal as it grows accustomed to eating solid food.

Once your boxer is an adult, you also have the option of making home cooked meals. The recommended ingredients among others are:

Lean chicken
Lamb
Veal
Turkey
Fish

This ingredient should make up 35 – 45 % of the meal. Next are the vegetables.

Sweet potatoes
Carrots
Cauliflower
Potatoes
String beans
Sweet peas

These ingredients should make up 25-35 % of the meal. Then add starch content to the mix in the form of rice or pasta.

Finish off with an excellent multivitamin or supplement (For dogs) and voila! You have a well fed, healthy, and happy pet.

Note: Not all of us have time to do home cooked meals for our pets. If you decide to purchase commercial dog food, take the time to find the healthiest alternative available and the most nutritious supplements for your pet.

Exercises

Remember: exercise is important to keep your Boxer occupied, and this can include:

-Breaking a sweat

Boxers need exercise and lots of it, even up to twice a day. So you can jog, run or walk briskly to get their blood flowing. (Note: This is a daily requirement, so if you unable to meet this type of demand on your time, a Boxer may not be the ideal pet for you)

-Socializing

Socialization is also important for this breed. So take the time to introduce your pet to other animals and people as well. If you are walking in a park or other social area, stop for a moment and help your dog to know it is all right to meet others.

-Running

Try to stay away from really hard surfaces. An open field (park area or similar site) is better since it is low impact on the frame of your pet. This will help their joints and feet to keep in tip top shape. Boxers can also adapt to apartment living.

Little girl with a Boxer puppy – Sharing a happy time

Living with the family

Children will love having a Boxer as a pet. They are great playmates for children and will interact well with other family pets. Of course to interact with family pets (Like other large dogs), there is a degree of socialization required, but it should not be too difficult.

Boxers enjoy the companionship of their human family, and they thrive on loving affection. If friends stop by, your pet may be distrustful, but it will melt away if they don't sense a threat to their loved ones.

It is not unusual for Boxers to do "tricks" for their owners. This could be a happy dance, funny sounds, or paw like movements just like a cat! This "clownish" behavior will delight you along with their "cuddly" antics.

If you are searching for the perfect happy, energetic and loyal companion, then a Boxer may just be the one for you!

 **Chapter 3**

Keeping it effective

This online article (***Dog Obedience Training Review***) encourages the following recommendations to train your pet. The best part of this training is how much fun it will be for both you and your pet to forge a strong bond, which will last a lifetime.

1- **Boxers are a handful**. This does not sound promising, but do not worry! Boxers are quick to learn and this makes it easier to get those training skills in motion. Easy terms such as sit, stay, fetch, down, etc… are learned very easily by Boxer puppies. Remember to train with love and affection and your dog will respond in kind.

2- ***Teach your Boxer to walk calmly on a leash.*** If you fail to take this step, this powerful and happy pet may drag you all over creation! That may not be fun, so start from early.

The following intriguing method is recommended:

-Hold the leash down at your waist.

-Walk much faster than usual, at first.

-Once your pet is used to your walking with a loose leash, repeat the technique in about 7 to 9 other locations. The dog will learn the lesson and automatically walk with a loose leash wherever you go!

Michele Welton from the website '*your pure bread puppy*' recommends the following training method. (This applies to all dog breeds and not just Boxers)

3 – *Try* **RESPECT TRAINING**. This is where you actually teach your pet to learn from **POSITIVE** and **NEGATIVE** consequences.

As a human we also learn from these same principles. For example: If we do something for someone and they say thank you, we may do it again. And yet if we forget to take out the garbage, and Daddy blows his top, more than likely we will not do it again. (At least we hope!)

Dogs, and in this case Boxers, learn in the same way. If our pet does something great we can reward it with smiles, hugs, laughs, kisses, games, treats, and whatever other happy outcome you will like. Trust me when I say Boxers will LOVE this!

On the other hand, if our pet does something we do not like we can transmit that with our voice, our look or use the leash or collar. It is important to note you will not hit, kick or otherwise abuse the animal. A simple tug with a firm voice is usually enough for the animal to figure out something is off.

This dignifies the dog and teaches it both respect and appreciation for boundaries. With loving attention and care, you can have a happy, obedient pet and a happy home.

So, what else can we learn about Boxers? Check out some amazing facts you may like to know!

- Boxers have a happy, energetic personality, but this does not mean they cannot get serious when required. They are used in the military and police force for their strength and courage. This work also extends to search and rescue and guard work.

- When it comes to being a watchdog, Boxers are hard to beat!

- Boxers have a lot of energy to release, so you need an active lifestyle to keep up with them. They do not do well being left on their own and can easily get depressed. This depressive behavior can turn destructive, so keep up healthy activities and your pet will thank you!

- Boxers are boisterous and love to jump on people. If this is one aspect of their personality that doesn't appeal to you, remember there are training skills to keep this type of behavior in check. You can ask a reputable veterinarian or professional what is the best way to train your Boxer in this regard.

- Boxers thrive on your loving affection, and will not hesitate to jump in your lap like a lapdog!

- Boxers can drool all over you and may snore a little too loud for your comfort. However, their devotion and sincere affection will soon have you forgetting about their slight imperfections!

-Male Boxers tend to be a bit laid back, but female Boxers are easily excited and quick to show their happiness.

- Boxers have a reputation of being a bit headstrong, but with loving attention and positive reinforcement, you can make your training successful.

So much fun!

FUN FACTS FOR KIDS:

Boxers have "Flashy" markings which are quite beautiful. Can you guess what this term means? Look at pictures of a Boxer and you will note white markings called "Flash" on their underbelly and feet. You can also research the color "Fawn" to find out what other colors apply to this term.

Do not forget to ask your parents or a guardian's permission before you search!

 # Conclusion

In conclusion:

Boxers have many qualities, which makes this pet ideal for a family home. Their clown like and boisterous nature is appealing to many, but this does not mean they are not intelligent. They are also excellent watchdogs, ideal guardians (in their own way), and eager to please you.

Their agility, strength, and stubbornness may be daunting at first, but with the proper socialization and training, their beautiful nature will shine.

Boxers are also versatile and have been used as messenger dogs in the military. Today we find them in many homes in different roles which include blind guide dogs, therapy dogs, and service dogs.

Despite their strength, Boxers are amazing with children and are ever patient and caring with them. Yes, sometimes they can get a bit excited and knock someone over, but they don't really mean it. This action only reflects the overwhelming happiness they feel to be your pet. They also possess an uncanny knack for knowing when you need loving attention, and are more than willing to provide it.

Ultimately, Boxers are everyone's best friend! If you decide to make this breed a part of your family home, you could not make a better choice than a fearlessly devoted and loving pet!

Author Bio

K. Bennett is a native from the Island of Roatan, North of Honduras. She loves to write about many different subjects, but writing for children is special to her heart.

Some of her favorite pastimes are reading, traveling and discovering new things. These activities help to fuel her imagination and act like a canvas for more stories.

She also loves fantasy elements like hidden worlds and faraway lands. Basically anything that gets her imagination soaring to new heights!

Her writing credits include local newspaper articles, a writing blog at Wordpress.com and other online stories. It also includes nonfiction books, children books online, and two novellas listed on Amazon.com

Download Free Books!
http://MendonCottageBooks.com

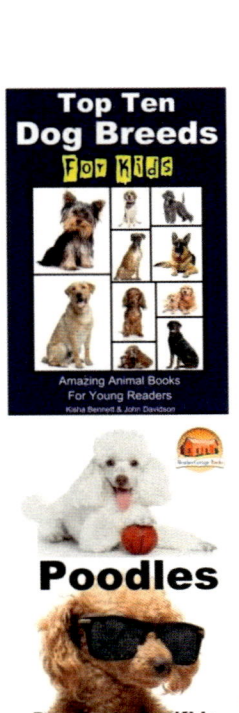

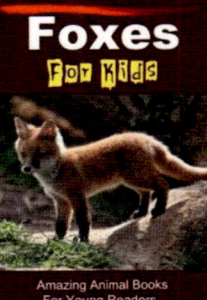

Our books are available at

1. Amazon.com

2. Barnes and Noble

3. Itunes

4. Kobo

5. Smashwords

6. Google Play Books

Download Free Books!
http://MendonCottageBooks.com

Publisher

JD-Biz Corp

P O Box 374

Mendon, Utah 84325

http://www.jd-biz.com/

Made in the USA
Monee, IL
23 January 2020